FOOL PROOF OUTLINE

A NO-NONSENSE SYSTEM FOR PRODUCTIVE PLANNING, OUTLINING, & DRAFTING NOVELS

CHRISTOPHER DOWNING

mad devil media

PART 1

WHAT TO EXPECT

A FEW QUICK NOTES

The best way to advance a writing career is to write and publish a lot of projects, whether you're into self-publishing or otherwise. The biggest obstacle to writing and publishing a lot of projects, however, is completing 1st Drafts. Of your first novel. Of every novel after.

Get the 1st Draft done, and you're more than 51% of the way there every time.

Most writers, unfortunately, abandon their projects before the 1st Draft is done. That's a bummer. Unfinished 1st Drafts leave you wondering about what could have been.

Then again, you don't want to waste your limited time muscling through a 1st Draft you don't believe has potential. That's a bummer too.

The Fool Proof Outline is here to help. It's going to solve both problems for you, the unfinished 1st Draft and the 1st Draft without potential. It's going to help you generate ideas, characters, plots, and settings that matter to you. It's going help keep you excited, keep you moving. In the end, it's going to keep readers reading.

You'll never know if your project has enough potential to edit and publish unless you knock out a 1st Draft, quickly and thoughtfully. Then, if you discover you no longer want to pursue it (which *does* happen), you can shelve it without too much time down the drain. Then, you dive into the next project. That's how the pros do it.

The reusable Fool Proof Outline will help you produce detailed, potential-filled 1st Drafts as quickly as possible. It contains questions and prompts that move you telescopically through story basics that burst with suspense and conflict, to characters that feel and breathe, to plots that make sense, and down to scenes with purpose. Best of all, there's an endpoint to the questions and prompts. You'll literally copy/paste your answers and ideas into a chronological outline. From there, you follow that outline, top to bottom, writing your 1st Draft.

That's great news for those of you figuring out your first novel.

Then, the more you reuse the Fool Proof Outline system, the better and faster you'll be. That's especially good news for those of us who write series.

For me, my next project on the white board is a seven book military space fantasy series. Think I want to waste time dabbling over characters and plots points that don't end up in the final cut? This is exactly why I built the Fool Proof Outline.

As an example, once I've made the outline for a scene, it takes me about 40 minutes to dictate a 1st Draft of that scene. Most of my 50k-word novels have ~40 scenes. Crunch the numbers. That means I'm writing a 50,000 word 1st Draft in less than 30 hours. *Not* non-stop, mind you. Even using my **Fool Proof Dictation** system, I can only manage three scenes a day before my brain turns to goo. Also, I'm a grateful full-time dad whose kids are 3 and 5. I get an hour and twenty minutes to write while the little one is in half-day preschool. Sometimes I manage to edit an hour after the kids go down. But that's it. Every. Minute. Counts.

That said, not everyone subscribes to the ***Write, Publish, Repeat*** mantra. That's fine too. The Fool Proof Outline contains enough brainstorming questions that if you're intentionally a slow writer, if you want to stew and percolate, tweaking ideas and characters, you'll have enough fodder to do that for months. Have at it. To each their own.

A lot of writing books break down the debate between outliners and pansters. If you want to delve into that debate, check them out. Me? I used to be a pantster, wasting lots of time and effort. Now I'm an outliner whose imagination explodes with ideas because I know what I'm looking for. That's to say, I'm a mega-mega outliner. You should be too.

If you're a diehard pantster? Good luck with that. You'll want to get your money back for this book sooner than later.

WHY SCRIVENER?

Because it's the best tool for what I do. It allows me to organize my ideas, so I can build a better, faster outline—and consequently a better, faster 1st Draft by simply cut/pasting those ideas directly into my text without changing windows.

I grabbed the free 30-day trial eighteen months ago, watched some how-to YouTube videos, and next thing you know, I published six books within a year under three pen names.

I don't have much incentive to jump ship now.

If you already drank the Scrivener Kool-Aid, you know its benefits and you know its potential. I hope the Fool Proof Outline realizes that potential for you.

If you're totally new to Scrivener, this is a fantastic way to learn what everyone's been going on about. Get the 30-day free trial. Follow this book. Fall in love.

You can always tweak the Outline, of course. Make it your own. If you do, drop me a line at scrivenertemplates@gmail.com. Let me know what works for you and what doesn't. The evolution from my last outlining system (published under The Ultimate Novel Template, no longer available) to the Fool Proof Outline was aided by feedback—positive and negative—from other writers. So keep me posted!

However, *I can't recommend exporting an ebook with Scrivener.* There are better ebook building tools there, such Vellum for Mac. I simply copy/paste my Final Draft from Scrivener into it. I know some people claim ebook formatting is a plus for Scrivener, but it's not perfect.

WHY EXCEL?

So truth is, I built my first reusable outline in Excel. From scratch. It was difficult to do. It kinda sucked.

I tried it in Word, too, for about twenty minutes before deciding it wouldn't organize things the way I needed.

Eventually, I realized I was trying to create an Excel workbook that organized ideas the same way Scrivener already did. Once I moved my outline over to Scrivener, life got easier.

That said, some people are resistant to Scrivener, so I backtracked for this book and built the Fool Proof Outline in Excel for them, and I think it works well. Let me know.

The Excel template still provides a format to view your ideas, questionnaires, and writing space all in one window. It's just divided into tabs along the bottom.

And no, sorry, there's still no Word version. Never will be. I simply couldn't make it work.

contains a place, Notes & Sketches, to do that. Later, if you keep them, cut/paste them into appropriate scenes.

Get the steps done as quickly as possible. That'll give you more time to circle back and tweak things, something you'll do a lot as characters and ideas thrive in your imagination.

Each step is loaded with questions that dig deep along the way, beginning with big picture stuff then focusing down to the little details. The questions have been crafted to elaborate story conflict, suspense, and character emotional depth—basically the stuff that keeps readers reading. They're the questions many writers forget to ask when they're wrapped up in the action of their story. *You* won't forget ever again because the questions are built into the Fool Proof Outline. You'll be happy with what they churn up for you.

During "Developing The Idea" and "Building Plot Structure," feel free to write as much as you want as answers, single sentences or a page. In the beginning, however, simple 2-4 sentence answers work best because they're easier to change and expand later, and they keep you from getting bogged down in the planning steps.

During "Developing Scenes," you'll need to limit your answers to a few lines because (and this is one of my favorite parts) you'll be copy/pasting those answers directly into your outline.

As we explore the steps of the Fool Proof Outline in this book, each chapter begins with a screenshot of that step's location within the application. That'll help guide you along the way.

I highly recommend you download the Scrivener or Excel template now. The web address is in the back of this book. Open it on your computer and follow along. Or if you're like me, read this book straight through, but explore the downloadable template soon after, while it's all fresh.

ABOUT THE PORTABLE DEVICE VERSIONS OF SCRIVENER AND EXCEL

Do phones and tablets work with the Fool Proof Outline?

Yes. Very well.

But I don't recommend using a portable device as you get to know the Fool Proof Outline.

I use the Fool Proof Outline on my phone all the time in the Scrivener app. But I'm already familiar with how the Outline is structured. My advice? Download the Scrivener or Excel template to your computer, get to know it, *then* transfer it to your device.

Some people write exclusively on their phones or tablets. If that's you, and you don't even have a laptop or desktop, this initial get-to-know-you phase will be tricky because the screen shots won't apply. But hang in there. As with most things associated with our portable devices, use, practice, and a little intuition usually save the day.

TEMPLATES WITHIN THE TEMPLATE

Whether you download the Scrivener template or the Excel template, there are smaller templates within each. I don't want you confused by terminology.

Writers comfortable with Scrivener will be right in their element. But users of Excel just need to remember most tabs within the downloadable workbook are smaller templates (a scene template, for instance) that need to be copied, renamed, and moved to their appropriate spot before working with them. Don't worry. We'll walk this process step-by-step throughout this book.

Below you'll see what the template folder looks like expanded in Scrivener. All the nuts and bolts that go into a solid novel. In one place. Waiting for you. So nice.

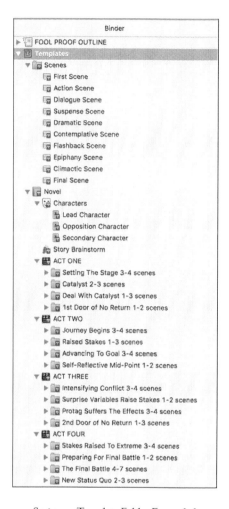

Scrivener Template Folder Expanded

Those of you using Excel, the templates are found as sheet tabs running from right to left. No way to get a screenshot of the group entirely.

Scrivener allows you to have template within template within template. For instance, you could add the "Novel" template, and the templates for acts, plot points, story brainstorm, and character worksheets will be contained within. Or you could merely add a new character worksheet. Or a single scene. Or all of Act Three.

You'll also see individual scene templates in both Scrivener and Excel versions (for example, Action Scene or Flashback Scene). I followed Jordan Rosenfeld's categories from her recommendable book *Make a Scene*. These scene templates—and the in-depth questionnaires within each—allow you to build plots and challenge your characters quickly. We'll break down each one as we use them.

Okay then.

Ready to brainstorm, outline, and draft a novel?

Scrivener users, change the name "Fool Proof Outline" to your own working title if you have one. Then, add the template "Novel" and open it up. Your Binder should look like this.

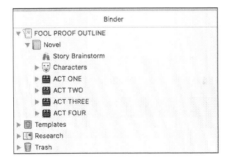

Excel users, your file is all ready to go. Read on.

It's time to start answering some questions.

PART 2

DEVELOPING THE IDEA

STORY BRAINSTORM

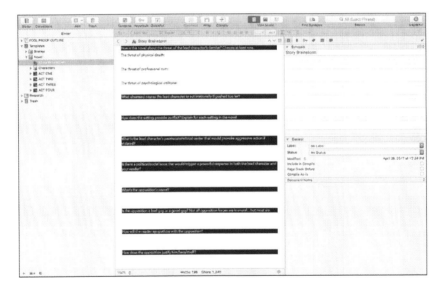

Story Brainstorm (Scrivener)

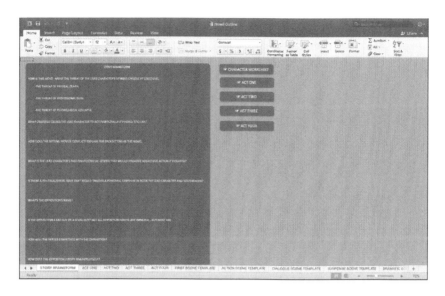

Story Brainstorm (Excel)

THE QUESTIONS

How is this novel about the threat of the lead character's demise? Choose at least one.

- **The threat of physical death:**
- **The threat of professional ruin:**
- **The threat of psychological collapse:**

Hands down, the best book I ever read on writing novels is James Scott Bell's **Plot & Structure**. *In it, he explains the idea of this first question at length. If you want readers to keep turning pages, you need to lure them with suspense. And you can't create suspense if danger isn't looming on every page. Even in the first chapter. Even in slow moving character-driven literary masterpieces, where pages need to drip with the protagonist's potential for psychological collapse.*

The three demises (JSB calls them "deaths") listed in this question are the most gripping. They will, therefore, evoke the strongest emotions from a reader. Which is your highest priority as a writer.

As with all questions, come back and modify them once you get to know your characters more, but jot down an initial idea. You're just brainstorming now. What major threat(s) will your protagonist face throughout the story?

What obsession causes the lead character to act irrationally if pushed too far?

You're going to come up with all sorts of conflict. Because that's what we like to read. And it propels characters toward change and action. So let's get to the extreme right away.

Even calm, little old ladies have a hot-button that'll get them fired up. And when people get fired-up, they often do things that don't make sense. It tells us a lot about a character.

How does the setting provide conflict? Explain for each setting in the novel.

You're not allowed to have boring settings. And being merely beautiful or interesting doesn't cut it. Don't waste your setting when it can cause trouble for your characters, even in ways that aren't completely obvious at the beginning. Every genre is capable of using environments that cause unsettling moments.

What is the lead character's passionate/ethical center that would provoke aggressive action if violated?

Not only are we looking for ways to create conflict, we're looking for ways to rally your characters into action. Give your protagonist something high and mighty to believe in—even before the story begins. Don't let your character walk onto the stage a blank moral canvas. That's boring. Give the reader something to agree with or disagree with. Either way, it's a starting place for change.

Is there a political/social issue that would trigger a powerful response in both the lead character *and* your reader?

Want to give your reader something to think about? Don't preach. You're above that. But figure out what issues of the day make your protagonist's stomach turn or blood boil. It's a level of reality and depth that's good for bonding readers to characters.

It's also a good way to get to know your protagonist.

What's the opposition's name?

The opposition might be ambiguous for the first half of the novel, but eventually, in order to have a satisfying climax, you need to get specific. It can be a person, a company, or a group of ethereal demons— but give it a name now.

Even if your novel is really about someone overcoming their fears and learning to love again, your readers will be happier if it happens while fighting something specific.

Is the opposition a bad guy or a good guy?

Not all opposition forces are immoral...but most are. It's worth thinking about.

How will the reader sympathize with the opposition?

Later in the character worksheets, you'll expand the deep wounds and fears of your opposition characters. Get a general idea now.

The opposition will lose The Final Battle of the final act. There's a lot of time before that happens for the reader to see things from the opposition's perspective. In fact, a powerful climax will tug the reader's heart strings when the opposition character is defeated. That might sound contradictory since the reader should be cheering the opposition's demise, but don't worry. Your reader can handle emotional contradictions. After all, readers are human. The alternative is a shallow, card-

board cutout, villainous archetype, but their defeat doesn't satisfy anyone.

How does the opposition justify him/hers/itself?

A good opposition is a strong opposition. A passionate opposition. An opposition fighting to its last dying breath. You don't need the reader sympathetic to the opposition's cause. It can be as dastardly and vile as you want. But you need to know why the opposition has taken taken this stance. What are his/her/its enthusiastic arguments for it.

Why is the opposition opposed specifically to the lead character?

Depending on the level of thrill and suspense you're after, the opposition will eventually begin gunning for your protagonist. At some point, your protagonist and opposition will be in a contest where there'll be only one winner.

The most riveting action-thrillers contain a moment when the protagonist had done something that makes the opposition morally committed to the protagonist's demise. Killed his relative. Stolen his prized golden chalice. Discredited his doctoral thesis.

It's a super way to raise the stakes anytime past the midpoint of the novel. At first, they wanted the same thing. Now, the opposition wants the protagonist dead.

At this point, you might notice more questions about the opposition than the protagonist. Not an accident. You may also be wondering why the heck I say opposition instead of antagonist the whole time. Yeah, I don't know. I just do.

Why can't the opposition and the lead character walk away from each other?

This is a great place to be creative. Sure, you can put them in a closed arena, throw in a knife, and lock the gates. But your story will be more intriguing if that arena is something intangible. Like a company. Or a cult. Or financial straits.

The characters could physically walk away, but something about who they are keeps them morally bound to the fight. You never want your reader asking, "Why doesn't she just leave town?"

What other characters contribute to the confrontation between the opposition and the lead character?

Common friends. Common enemies. An ally egging on the lead character inappropriately. Most characters in the novel will eventually contribute to the novel's primary conflict, even if it's not apparent in the beginning. Just start brainstorming about it now.

Summarize The Final Battle:

Scenes of the climax will burst with the greatest emotional intensity of the entire novel. You need to be thinking about it from day one. You need to be picturing it in your head. You need to be working everything toward it. It's kind of a big deal.

You don't need to know all The Final Battle's details to start a novel, but you need to start working on them, getting excited about them.

The Final Battle depends a lot on genre expectations. You should know what those are from reading countless books in your genre. (You do read your genre, right?) If anything, summarize what those genre expectations are for a climax. But eventually, a half page summary of your novel's climax will do wonders by giving you a goal to work towards.

Why are the stakes at their highest during The Final Battle?

This ties right back into the first question. It's all jeopardized during the climax. Make it or break it.

If you want readers chewing through their cuticles, The Final Battle needs to be about more than bragging rights. All the personal growth will slip away. All the children will go back to the orphanage. All the rebels will be hung at noon. All the tears will be for nothing.

Figure out what's the most over-the-top way the world would suffer if the protagonist lost The Final Battle. Then, work backwards. You'll do this in more detail when we tackle the major plot points later.

BEFORE YOU GO ON

Again, in any of the questionnaires, it's okay to merely make a few notes as answers. I recommend you come back through and re-examine your ideas, however, especially as you're constructing the plot. Keep asking yourself these questions. Keep coming back to challenge yourself as you plan your novel. In the end, you'll be challenging your lead character most, and that, I promise, will make for a better novel.

CHARACTER WORKSHEETS

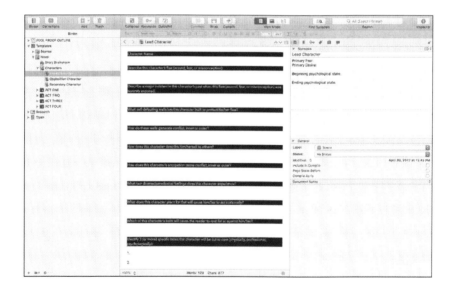

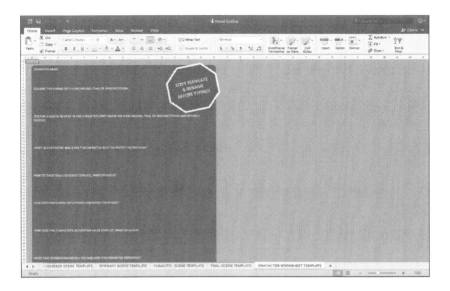

Character worksheets are the same for lead characters, opposition characters, and even secondary characters. These few questions will help you create people with compelling emotional complexity.

You'll notice this worksheet doesn't worry about character facts that don't bring depth to the story. Even "Appearance Basics" is listed at the bottom. By using the following prompts, you can branch out and expand as much as you need, especially for the lead and opposition characters. Start with short, simple answers if you want. Come back later.

We know small things have enormous effects on the lives of characters. So we're not excluding small things. We're excluding trivial things. There's a difference.

Even if your novel is full of *Seinfeld*-esque banter, the unspoken subtext needs to be rich with character motivations, fears, and flaws. Life's funnier that way.

Want extra credit? Fill this questionnaire out for yourself. Did it hit on the heavy stuff? The important stuff you wished more people cared about?

THE QUESTIONS

Character Name

Spending too much time on character names is like spending too much time playing with fonts in your manuscript. Peruse novels in your genre. Search for popular names in the time period. Make it easy to pronounce. Move on.

Describe this character's flaw (wound, fear, or misconception).

This is the most important aspect to nail down in the whole story. Take it seriously. All the various ways you elucidate this character flaw, all the ways you show the character stifled by it, all the ways you pour salt on it, and finally, all the ways you celebrate the character overcoming it will fuel the emotional experience for the reader.

Whether you're developing a good guy or a bad guy, there's something major preventing the character from living life fully. It could be a wounded heart. It could be a deeply rooted fear, such as a dread of being worthless, of being alone, of being helpless. It could be a misconception, like the belief that fascism is awesome.

Every character has a significant flaw (or two). It will affect nearly every desire and decision that matters to the story. So don't hide it from the reader. You don't need to hammer anyone over the head with it, either. Use subtext like a good writer. Use scenes of high tension to let the flaw flop out in an irrational way for all to see.

The lead character will need to face that flaw. If you construct a strong plot, the lead character will need to overcome that flaw to overcome the opposition in The Final Battle.

Truth is, our flaws steer our actions more than our high-minded principles. Especially during hard times. And guess what, your entire novel is about your protagonist going through hard times. So there you go.

Describe a major incident in this character's past when this flaw (wound, fear, or misconception) was severely exposed.

You need to give your character good reasons for not fixing his/her flaw. If we were all logical beings, we'd identify our issues and correct them. However, reality reveals us denying or even nurturing our flaws. The bigger the flaw, the more we allow it to define us. And if that flaw is exposed in a horrifying, traumatizing, embarrassing way, we actually cling to it more.

I know, right? Humans are so weird.

Think of a pre-story experience that gives your character a reason not to fix his/her flaw. Not the cause of the flaw itself, mind you. But a time when that flaw was put under the light. If your character is obsessed by embarrassment of his childhood poverty, then think of a time when that embarrassment became a public humiliation, as a child or even later as a wealthy adult.

You don't need to use it as a full flashback scene, but you can. You can artfully reference it occasionally whenever the character is faced with the flaw, the wound, fear, or misconception. You'll want to explain it fully to the reader eventually, but you can tease it out as the plot progresses.

What self-defeating walls has this character built to protect his/her flaw?

Not only do we find ways to covet our flaws, we find ways to keep others from messing with them. We build walls. We become reclusive. We develop bad tempers. We defy authority. We exaggerate our vanities. We act impulsively. We talk sarcastically. We steal from the collection plate so no one will expect us to be nice.

These walls need to come down by the time The Final Battle occurs.

How do these walls generate conflict, inner or outer?

There are the consequences to our self-defense mechanisms. These are the details making things ludicrously complex. But also closer and closer to reality. A wife is so consumed with the fear that her husband will cheat on her that she resorts to destructive passive-aggressive behavior, thus driving him away. That sort of thing.

Think of a few examples for your characters. Come back to this later too.

How does this character describe him/herself to others?

Your character puts on a mask every time he/she walks out the front door. You do, too, by the way. It's not always a bad thing. But it can be.

Conflict, tension, and irrational behavior cause the mask to fall off. It's exciting to see what's really underneath. Of course, booze does this. But that's cheating.

How does this character's occupation cause conflict, inner or outer?

Does anyone have a conflict-free job? Explore the many ways your character experiences occupational tension—even if your character isn't an FBI agent on the prowl.

The frustrations we feel at work are a really big deal to us. Maybe not to anyone else. But work drama, even the mundane stupid drama, often permeates our thoughts.

Not that we want to involve the reader with mundane drama. But it's worth looking into depending on the needs of your novel.

What two diverse/paradoxical feelings does this character experience?

You'll want go beyond the primary emotions of rage, grief, terror, ecstasy, admiration, vigilance, amazement, and loathing. If those are your only target emotions, your novel will feel shallow—even if you slather those emotions on every page. So don't do that.

A realistic character will experience secondary and tertiary emotions at any given time. Even ones seeming to contradict the primary one.

Someone can long to save humanity but also feel annoyed by specific things about people.

A policeman can hate a criminal while feeling distracted by administrative bureaucracy at the exact same time. He might even say, "Screw it," let the bad guy go, and then hate himself for it later.

For my own novels, I keep the image of Plutchik's Emotion Wheel handy while I outline at the scene level. I use it to brainstorm lesser emotions a character might feel at any given time. Then, I weave that lesser emotion into the subtext of a scene. Sometimes my scenes will focus on the lesser emotion and entirely ignore the obvious primary emotion. Good stuff. Gives the reader something to chew on. I got the idea from sleeping with Raymond Carver's short stories under my pillow.

What does this character yearn for that will cause him/her to act irrationally?

Be specific. Pick something obtainable, even physically tangible. Even if it's a long shot for the character. Winning a specific contest. A date with Miss Hotty Hotterson. A high-profile law case. Revenge for a father's death.

This isn't the primary objective of the novel, however. Make the craving something that's been a part of the character long before the story begins. Funny and quirky. Self-destructive and morbid.

Dangle it in front of your character throughout the story. Then, let his/her behavior surprise the reader.

Me? I'm always on the lookout for two things: chocolate and quiet time. Both of which I rarely get these days. But tease me with them. Then, watch me get really, really awkward if you try taking them away.

Which of this character's traits will cause the reader to root *for or against* him/her?

Nothing complicated here.

If this is your protagonist, you want the reader rooting for him/her. So make sure the character has some endearing qualities. Even if the protagonist has a lot to learn at the beginning, there needs to be some way for the reader to know he/she is a good person.

If this is an opposition character, consider whether you want him/her to quietly drift away or go up in a big, gnarly ball of flames. If it's the latter, the reader should be on board that this was the right thing to do.

Identify 3 (or more) specific times this character will be cut to core (physically, professional, psychologically):

1.

2.

3.

This is beginning to veer into plot building.

Start visualizing scenes where very bad things happen your characters. Even the opposition. Even the secondary characters.

Think about the most primal desires and fears of your characters. How can you specifically hurt them there. And hurt them bad.

Think about that flaw (wound, fear, or misconception). You've already imagined a time earlier in their lives when that flaw caused major emotional trauma. Make them relive it.

You can also simply have someone kick the crap out of them. That's definitely not cheating. No one really likes that.

Appearance Basics:

Don't forget to give the reader something to picture in their heads. Keep it simple.

PART 3

BUILDING PLOT STRUCTURE

ACT ONE

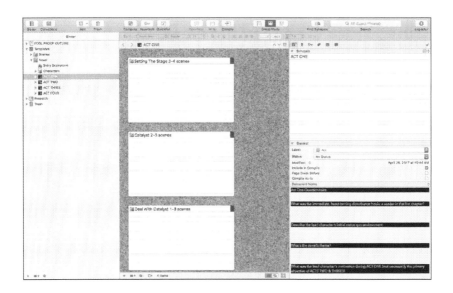

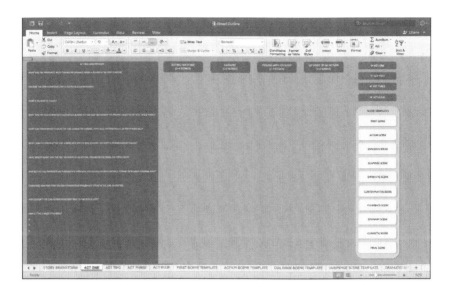

SCRIVENER NOTE

Each act is a folder. The questionnaires for each act are found in Inspector, in the document notes. When I'm using Inspector, I widen it as much as I can. It's a legitimate workspace, and I like plenty of elbow room to move around. Portable device users navigate to Inspector via the little "i" at the bottom of the screen.

EXCEL NOTE

Each act is a self-contained sheet. You see the major plot points lined up left to right. Later on, you'll be cut/pasting scene synopses under them.

ACT ONE QUESTIONNAIRE

What was the immediate, head-turning disturbance that hooks a reader in the first chapter?

Your novel's first job is to make the reader turn from page one to page two. Something serious needs to be in there. It doesn't need to be world-wrecking, but it needs to excite the reader. It should also give the reader a taste of what's to come.

Even if your novel isn't a techno-thriller, it'll do its job better if something is wrong in the first pages. And seeing what's wrong from the protagonist's POV will immediately give the reader insights into him/her.

Waste your reader's time, and they won't turn the page. Plant tension right off the bat, and they'll get sucked in.

So brainstorm something that can go wrong, even something minor, that conveys as much subtextual information as possible about the protagonist's world.

Describe the lead character's initial status quo environment:

Your protagonist will be making some drastic changes. What's life like when the novel starts?

Most importantly, think about the character worksheet you made for the protagonist. Think about those flaws and fears and desires. How do they play out in the protagonist's world at the novel's beginning? Think of a few examples that show (not tell) him/her experiencing those flaws and fears and desires in that world.

What's the novel's theme?

Another job of the first few chapters is to let the reader know the novel's meaning. That's theme.

Theme is a statement. Not a question. Not a recurring motif. Love conquers all. Blood is thicker than water. Every student matters. Life sucks, then you die.

Stay away from multiple themes. Pick one for the reader to identify, to mull over.

Challenge the theme throughout the novel. Make the reader think you've given up on your statement just before the last act. Then, champion it. How you do that is up to you. But your reader should be able to tell their friends your novel had meaning, even if it's a grimdark fantasy.

Consider challenging your theme in the first chapter. In fact, your theme needs to be challenged or championed in almost every scene. Subtly, sure, but it should be there.

What was the lead character's motivation during ACT ONE (not necessarily the primary objective of ACTS TWO & THREE)?

Give your protagonist a goal from the get go, perhaps one ongoing as the novel opens. That goal should reveal a lot about the character and his/her beginning environment, even if it's comically trivial. He/she can achieve the goal or fail miserably. Guess which is more revealing and entertaining.

What was threatening to cause the lead character's demise, physically, professionally, or psychologically:

This should be familiar.

We're not talking anything to do with the opposition. Yet. Could be, though. Act One is about more than setting the stage for future conflict. It needs its own conflict. Whether that conflict connects to the rest of the novel is up to you.

What catalyst shook up the lead character's status quo, starting the novel's progression of change?

Some say catalyst. Some people say inciting incident. I like catalyst because of the expression "catalyst for change." Because that's what your novel is about.

It's the spark that starts the story going. Like discovering an ancient map in the attic. Like a spaceship landing in the middle of the city. Like a new ranch hand coming to town.

It needs to be significant enough to create a dilemma for the protagonist. Will she start a valiant quest to discover what treasure the map leads to? Maybe. Maybe not. Home sure is cozy.

What specific event was the First Doorway of No Return, irrevocably altering the status quo?

James Scott Bell calls this plot point in Act One the 1st Doorway of No Return because it's the point where the protagonist cannot retreat back to the safety of the old status quo. The only way to go is forward.

The protagonist must identify the new primary objective, then be committed to it completely.

The world can make the choice for your reluctant protagonist, shoving him/her through the door into the rest of the plot by dire circumstance. However, a more interesting character is one who's an active agent of change. Making tough decisions. Sticking her neck out there even early on.

Think of a specific action that commits the protagonist to the adventure. Make sure the reader knows exactly what it means as it happens. Make sure everyone, including your protagonist, knows there's no going back. Only forward.

Why did the lead character go through this doorway, voluntarily or involuntarily, thereby increasing personal risk?

You need to be able to articulate this from the protagonist's perspective.

Bonus round: what if the protagonist's initial reasons are part of an emotional self-defense mechanism? Part of a big self-deception? Later he/she'll need to discover why he/she's really doing all this.

Summarize how this event caused introspection and/or self-doubt in the lead character:

This is pretty obvious. If you make a huge commitment, you're going to experience some strong feelings. Doubt. Excitement. Fight or flight. While this is no dark night of the soul—which comes later—let the reader know how this commitment is a shake up.

Why couldn't the lead character retreat back to the status quo?

Work this out, being as specific as possible.

How do the subplots progress?

1.

2.

3.

4.

If your novel contains subplots, number them. Keep track of them. Don't let them get sloppy.

ACT TWO

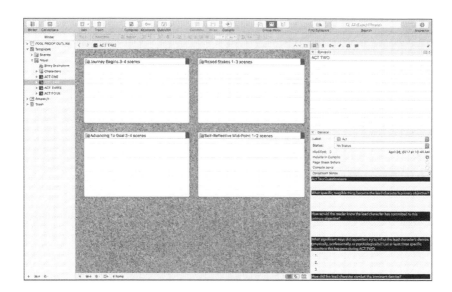

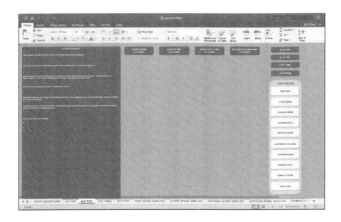

ACT TWO QUESTIONNAIRE

What specific, tangible thing became the lead character's primary objective?

The reader will want a clearly defined goal by Act Two. Make sure your novel spells it out well. That way, the reader will be able to judge your protagonist's actions here on out. And the reader will better appreciate the nasty setbacks along the way.

No aimless wandering. Unless you're writing an experimental art novel.

Don't write an experimental art novel.

How would the reader know the lead character has committed to this primary objective?

From here on out, most scenes should be about the protagonist pursuing the primary objective.

The protagonist is past the 1st Doorway of No Return, but he/she needs to occasionally reconfirm his/her commitment to the reader. Maybe it's just a verbal statement. Preferably it's taking steps forward that are painful and difficult.

If you want the reader to bond emotionally with your protagonist, make sure they're on the same page.

What significant ways did opposition try to inflict the lead character's demise (physically, professionally, or psychologically)? List at least three specific occasions this happens during ACT TWO:

1.

2.

3.

A lot depends how well defined the opposition is at this point. But by the middle of the novel, the protagonist needs to have already suffered some hard knocks. Maybe from the opposition. Maybe from the opposition's agent. Depends how mano a mano *you want your novel to be.*

The question mentions the 3 threats you came up with at the beginning of the "Story Brainstorm." They're handy to have around. Think of ways to gradually increase those threats.

How did the lead character combat the imminent demise?

Brainstorm your protagonist's skill set. Make a list. How can he/she defend herself. Or even fight back.

Summarize how the lead character confronted his/her own flaw (wound, fear, or misconception) during the threats of the imminent demise:

Remember in the "Character Worksheet" when we talked about flaws and masks and going through hard times. Until your character overcomes his/her flaw in the final act, that flaw will keep making things difficult—and emotionally messy. That's good story stuff.

Conflict and tension on the higher end of the scale will bring up things he/she won't want to confront. It's your job as the writer to make sure it happens.

During a major self-reflective moment, what does the lead character learn about him/herself that must change in order to achieve the primary objective?

By the end of Act Two, life isn't much fun. If you've been doing your job, your protagonist will have begun dredging the quagmire of emotions.

Brainstorm an epiphany scene when your protagonist faces the possibility that his/her flaw must be overcome in order to achieve the primary objective. He/she probably doesn't foresee The Final Battle yet. The scene can be dark, action-filled, or full of sniveling puppies.

There can be hope at the end of the scene too. It depends on the personality of your lead character. Readers like hope.

The question becomes for the rest of the novel, what will the lead character do with that epiphany. Keep building walls around the heart? Or dive to the bottom of the quagmire?

Whatever your protagonist decides, things are going to get a heckuva lot worse in Act Three. And remember, there's no going back.

James Scott Bell wrote an entire book about this moment, **Write Your Novel From The Middle**. *Although it doesn't suggest four acts, this book is the main reason I use a four act structure. The plot point I call the Emotional Mid-point is so significant it cleaves a story in half. Everything in the first half leads up to the Emotional Mid-point, and everything in the second half cascades away from it. Basically, I took an axe to the typically long Act Two of a three act drama and split it down the middle.*

How do the subplots progress?

1.

2.

3.

4.

Think of ways your subplots can actively influence your primary plot. Vice versa too. Especially if they complicate each other, making life more difficult for everyone.

ACT THREE

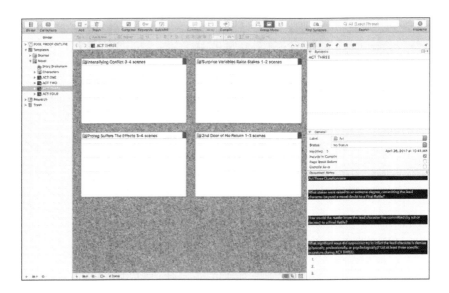

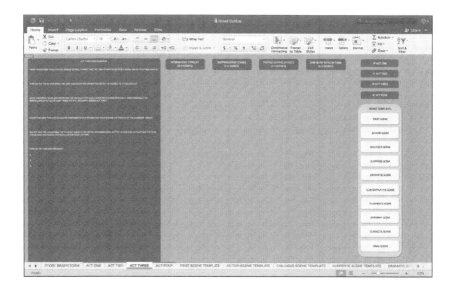

ACT THREE QUESTIONNAIRE

What stakes were raised to an unexpectedly high degree, committing the lead character beyond a moral doubt to a Final Battle?

This part of the novel is about making things truly awful for your protagonist. All the personal threats, the possible demises, the inflamed flaws, they're all going to get the major smack down. Just about everything that could go wrong will go wrong.

Near the end of Act Three (in a four act story), your protagonist will realize the only way to survive is fighting the opposition directly. But losing that fight will guarantee the demise(s) you considered at the beginning of "Story Brainstorm." You're going to be setting that up in Act Three.

If your protagonist decides to cross the 2nd Doorway of No Return toward The Final Battle of the last act, death and/or catastrophic defeat is not only a real possibility, it's likely.

Your protagonist will make the right choice, of course. He/she will make the conscious decision to put it all on the line and go to The Final Battle.

How would the reader know the lead character has committed (by act or decree) to The Final Battle?

Unlike the 1st Door of No Return, where your protagonist can be reluctantly shoved through, this time the decision has to be a deliberate. Probably a lonely, existential one.

What action shows your protagonist committed to The Final Battle?

What serves as the closed door preventing any desperate retreat?

What significant ways did opposition try to inflict the lead character's demise (physically, professionally, or psychologically)? List at least three specific occasions during ACT THREE:

1.

2.

3.

The questions are the same from Act Two. This time, however, your answers need to involve significant, specific effort by the opposition to crush the protagonist. Let the evil side really do its job. Don't hold back. Make Act Three a ferocious sprint through hell. No one will be mad if your novel is too awesome.

Summarize how the lead character confronted his/her own existence during the threats of this imminent demise:

In the major self-reflective moment of Act Two, the protagonist realized how detrimental his/her major flaw is. The continuing threats and setbacks of Act Three show how the character is changing.

Even as life gets harder and uglier, your protagonist should begin dealing with that flaw. It shouldn't heal overnight, after all.

Restate why the lead character couldn't morally avoid the impending Final Battle? In doing so, explain how the lead character's emotional experience differs from ACT ONE.

What would happen if your protagonist actually gave up? What if the temptation to maintain those walls around the wounded heart was too strong?

Tempt your protagonist with the old status quo. Sometimes people stay in abusive relationships because it's all they know. That's powerful stuff.

Not only that, during Act Three, your protagonist has been working on his/her flaw, and life has only gotten worse. What kind of crap is that? Seriously. Near the end of Act Three, your protagonist will be in a very dark place—for good reason. Take your time. Explore that dark place.

And yet...

...he/she will still summon the courage to forge ahead.

Because it's the righteous thing to do.

How do the subplots progress?

1.

2.

3.

4.

Don't let those snarky subplots get away from you. You're the boss. Start pinning down how they're going to wrap up.

ACT FOUR

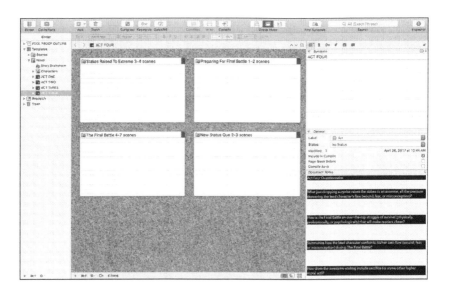

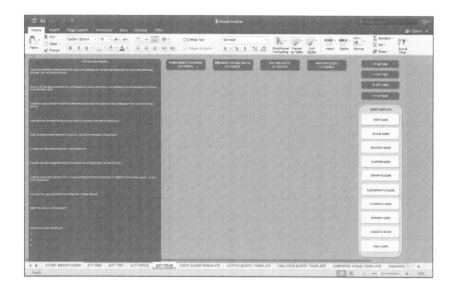

ACT FOUR QUESTIONNAIRE

What jaw-dropping surprise raises the stakes to an extreme, all the pressure skewering the lead character's flaw (wound, fear, or misconception)?

Just when your protagonist thought he/she knew all the risks, committing to the life and death battle to come, you raise the stakes to a degree that no one saw coming. Like, you need to surprise everyone, including the reader, with an extra layer of agony.

It should be aimed directly at your protagonist's major flaw. Don't worry about going over the top. You can't. As long as you stay within your genre, you can't make the stakes too high.

Most writers actually begin to feel sorry for their characters at this point and hold back. It's true. But that's not what readers want you to do. And they're your customer. Give them more than they paid for. Make them say, "Holy hell!"

Sometimes the The Final Battle is a continuation of the protagonist's primary objective. But sometimes, the protagonist obtains his/her primary objective at the end of last act, either causing the opposition to obsess over the destruction of the protagonist or causing an unexpected showdown. And if I were your opposition character, I'd go right for your protagonist's weak spot: the flaw.

How is The Final Battle an over-the-top struggle of survival (physically, professionally, or psychologically) that will make readers cheer?

In a culmination of all the conflict, tension, and emotional grind, The Final Battle is the point of your novel's highest intensity. It's good to articulate why the reader will feel that. Practice saying it, and you'll make sure you have a solid understanding how everything that's come before leads unequivocally to this event.

Summarize how the lead character confronts his/her own flaw (wound, fear, or misconception) during The Final Battle?

Let's say your lead character has been looking for ways to deal with his/her flaw all through Act Three. Now with Act Four comes the realization those ways haven't been working. On some level, your lead character has still been secretly clinging to the hope that the walls around the wounded heart, all those self-defense mechanisms, will get to stay up after the adventure is over.

To make things worse, it turns out the only way to win The Final Battle involves facing the true reality of the flaw and finally overcoming it.

Work that into your story. If it ties together, it'll make for a great climax.

Once you have this down, work backwards toward the beginning of the story, keeping this in mind, making sure the flaw and the The Final Battle have a final conclusion that work together.

How does the awesome ending include sacrifice (or some other higher moral act)?

Including a significant sacrifice in the The Final Battle is a great way rally the emotions. Brainstorm other noble deeds to tie into Act Four.

Does the ending make sense? Is it a sensical last step of the novel's progression?

Sometimes you need to step back. Make sure you're not forcing characters to do things they wouldn't do. Make sure the reader can, if only in hindsight, say the The Final Battle felt inevitable.

Is there anything predictable that can be removed?

When you step back, it's also worth looking for predictability. Writing to genre expectations is good. Writing a predictable ending is bad.

Describe the lead character's new status quo environment once the dust settled:

Create a new situation for your protagonist, but compare it, at least here, to the initial status quo of Act One. How is the world different from back then?

Describe an incident showing that the lead character's flaw (wound, fear, or misconception) is now healed—or is at least in recovery:

Writing a least a few scenes about life after the adventure does a few important things. Don't skimp. Plan them well.

Firstly, it gives the reader a chance to breathe after the climax. If you've done a good job, the reader doesn't want the story to end, so use that time to wrap up all those emotions you evoked. Here's your chance to make a last impression, a wonderful "Aahhh" moment. And, if we're being honest, the last pages of this novel are absolutely, posi-

tively, undeniably the best marketing for your next novel. So I'll say it again: don't skimp.

Secondly, your protagonist gets to show the reader that things have really changed. Overcoming the flaw wasn't a fluke. Wasn't a one-time deal. You can be subtle how you show it, but the reader should see the protagonist actively doing something, even something small, showing the flaw is either healed or is on the way to being healed. It's a feel good moment, yes, and since the reader has been there with you the whole time, they deserve to feel good.

How will the last paragraph in the book nail a "wow" feeling?

Speaking of last impression, brainstorm what that will be. What's it going to take to do that?

Draft the novel's last paragraph:

Some writers (not many) compose the last paragraph first. Doesn't mean you'll stick to it. But, just like knowing The Final Battle before you begin writing, knowing the final feelings you'll be leaving your reader with helps pull you along during the writing process.

Try it. You never know.

How do the subplots resolve?

1.

2.

3.

4.

No subplot left behind! You must conclude every subplot. All of them. You must, you must, you must.

Unless you're writing a series. Okay, then you don't have to.

MAJOR PLOT POINTS

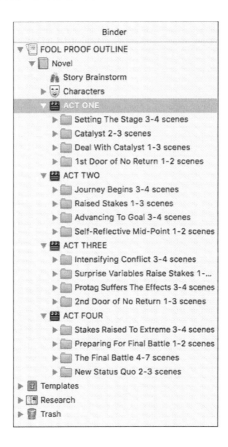

Here's a screenshot of the acts expanded in Scrivener, showing the plot points. Excel users will see plot points laid out across the top of each act.

Each plot point (a.k.a. story beat) moves the story through increasingly difficult predicaments, higher stakes, and consequently more emotional intensity.

Each plot point has its own buildup and climax. The next plot point starts off calmer, giving the reader some breathing room, then it ratchets up toward its own peak scene.

You'll see that I suggest an amount of scenes for each plot point. Take it or leave it, but beginner writers can see an approximate amount of space to devote.

Some novels skip certain plot points altogether. You can, for instance, jump into the catalyst on page one, skipping the set up. Why not? You can do whatever you want. A longer novel will use all of the plot points. A shorter one will leap frog others.

I suggest you use all of them. Even in a 40k-word novel. **The plot structure of the Fool Proof Outline is already set up to satisfy readers in the most reliable, time-tested way possible.** If you don't change any of the plot points, you'll be on your way to success. Not only are they safe for you, they're exciting for readers. Not only does the Hero's Journey fit, but I was able to apply them to all twenty of Ronald Tobias's *20 Master Plots*.

Up to this point, most of the answers you've been working on have given you what you need for each plot point. Your protagonist needs to struggle toward the primary objective. Also, remember in the questionnaires for acts one & two, when you answered *What significant ways did opposition try to inflict the lead character's demise (physically, professionally, or psychologically)?* Work with those answers.

Rename each plot point in the outline to signify what happens in each. Feel free to use short sentences or simple phrases, similar to the title of a chapter. You can also leave the default title at the end of your new name, so you remember what plot point it's supposed to represent.

Now you've got a preliminary idea of what happens at each step within each act.

At this point in the process, I'd let the brainstorming settle for a little bit before moving on. If you haven't yet, review all the questionnaires and prompts up to this point, over and over until you have complete confidence in the story.

This is where you know whether your story has potential. It should. But if you feel uneasy about something, keeping reviewing and reworking your answers. Something in your heart will click when everything makes sense, when all the acts line up cohesively, when your characters begin demanding that you start writing blood into their veins.

Also, this a time when scene ideas start exploding into existence in your mind. As you review your ideas from "Developing The Idea" and "Building Plot Structure," specific moments in the story will begin to pop up. Jot those moments down in Notes & Sketches. Don't worry about writing full scenes. Sometimes it's nothing more than list of irresistible ideas you want to include at some point. You will have lots of time later to flush out scene details. Frankly, this is one of the most exciting times in the novel writing process. Enjoy it.

When you're ready, or your imagination tapers off, move on to the next step. In it, you'll be figuring out which scenes serve each plot point best. More fun.

PART 4

DEVELOPING SCENES

A NOTE ON SCENES

Here's an overview of how to fill the Fool Proof Outline with scenes:

- Identify the goal and climax moment of each plot point.
- Identify the types of scenes you want in that plot point.
- Create a compact synopsis of each scene, including the opening, peak emotional moment, and the ending.
- Review a scene's checklist.
- Answer a scene's "Scene Basics" questionnaire.
- Copy/paste your answers as a scene's chronological outline.

After that, you knock out your 1st Draft.

Another advantage of the Fool Proof Outline is its bundle of scene templates. Need an action scene? A suspense scene? A dialogue scene? There's templates for each. The checklist for each type of scene is different too because each type serves a different purpose. The "Scene Basics" questionnaire, however, is almost exactly the same for them all.

Now's a great time to explore the Scrivener or Excel file, especially if you've been putting it off until now. Check out the scene templates within. The more familiar you are with them now, the smoother your progression from here.

TO USE TEMPLATES OR NOT TO USE TEMPLATES?

You can guess where I sit on this question.

Some people say templates don't belong in the creative process. Okay. Some people say they prefer not getting bogged down with the burden of act structure (3 or 4 acts, or whatever). Fine.

For me, it's about meeting and exceeding reader expectations, even at the scene level. Templates serve as a guide to reader expectations. In a way, they set me free. When I know the right structure I'm working within, whether it's acts or scenes, my imagination becomes fearless. Ideas come faster. My inner critic shuts up. Writing time becomes more productive.

Freedom through structure. What do you say to that?

Sounds like a way to sell more good books, that's what I say.

FILLING OUT PLOT POINTS

Check out these screenshots:

Scene Ideas Within Plot Points (Scrivener)

Scene Ideas Within Plot Points (Excel)

Your plot points move the story from act to act. Then, your scenes move the story from plot point to plot point. Like connecting the dots.

In the examples above, I inserted scene ideas into each of the four plot points of Act One, a story (I just made it up) about a woman reluctantly thrust into a small town labor war.

Go through each act of your novel. Look at the plot points. Think of scenes that will logically connect the dots. Write them in plot points as I did in the examples. Keep in mind all the macro-lens ideas you brainstormed earlier. If you already have scene ideas sketched in Notes & Sketches, can you find a place where they work?

This is another fun part of the Fool Proof Outline. Your imagination is free to generate fun, emotionally driven scene ideas without much commitment to time or effort. You're not even writing full sentences. Explore as many routes between the dots as you can. Nothing is set in stone.

Excluding the first and last plots points in the novel (Setting the Stage & The New Status Quo), every plot point ends in its own climax. The first scenes of a plot point lead to a scene of peak intensity, the last scene of a plot point. You'll see that in my example above.

Make sure plot points progress logically. Even if you're keeping important information from the reader, such as a mystery/thriller, they need to make sense at least in hindsight. Cause and effect. Action and consequence. This sounds obvious to some, but tons of novels are riddled with plot holes. Linking your plot points with cause and effect will help eliminate plot holes. The Fool Proof Outline lines up your plot points, giving you an advantage to reduce such gaffes.

At the same time, if you have scene ideas already in the works, you can identify where they fit.

You *must* let go of scene ideas that don't fit in the cause and effect pattern of your plot points. No matter how much you love them. No matter how beautifully you wrote the scene sketch. If you must, find a way to weave the idea into another scene that does belong. New writers often allow scenes that don't propel the plot forward because it's difficult to "kill your darlings." But your readers will appreciate it. I promise. Auxiliary scenes may be pretty, but they're not the story. Readers suck the marrow out of pages that show what happens next in the story. They skim pages that don't.

At this point in the Fool Proof Outline, you have most of your scenes identified. That means your novel is plotted. Congratulations. As always, you're free to add or subtract later.

Revisit the Story Brainstorm and all the Character Worksheets. Did you hit all your ideas? Did you think of scenes that allow those ideas to happen? Or did you alter some of your original ideas during plotting? Update those questionnaires if you've altered course and you like where you went. Keep your outline and your questionnaires in sync. Sometimes valuable ideas get lost on their way from the brainstorm to the outline. Stay on top of them all the way through the process.

PACING & SCENE TYPES

Ask yourself how you want each scene to feel. Action-oriented. Suspenseful. Dramatic. Fast. Slow.

At this point in the process, establish the pacing of the novel. Contemplative scenes will read slower than dialogue scenes. Dialogue scenes read slower than action scenes. Pacing is part genre expectations, part artistic license.

In Scrivener, add scene templates within plot points, as shown in the example below. Begin feeling out the pace of your novel. This is easier to do the more you use the scene templates, but begin playing around.

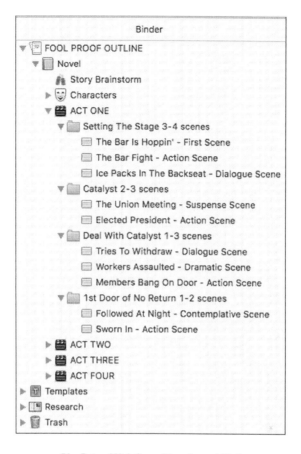

Plot Points With Scene Templates Added

In Excel, the process is more time consuming. Navigate to the tab for a scene template you want, right-click/copy, moving the template just after the appropriate act tab. That is, between the tabs for Acts One and Two if the new scene is in Act One. You're going to have a long line of tabs running along the bottom of your window, but the navigation buttons in each sheet will significantly help.

Finally, if scene types confuse you, we'll go over each briefly soon.

SCENE SYNOPSES

Contemplative Scene

[insert a 1 sentence scene summary, incl. POV's objective]

WHO:
WHERE:
TIME & WEATHER:

OPENING:

PEAK EMOTIONAL MOMENT:

ENDING:

Scene Synopsis Card (Scrivener)

Scene Synopsis Text Box (Excel)

In keeping with the Fool Proof Outline's progression from big picture to smaller details, flesh out each scene with the scene synopses. Each scene synopsis card has 7 prompts.

Let's go over each:

[Insert a 1 sentence scene summary, incl. POV's objective]

Every scene should have a well-defined purpose, so well-defined you can express it in a single sentence. If you can't do it in a single sentence, maybe you're dealing with two scenes crammed together.

Stay at it until you can do it. The process will crystalize the scene for you.

WHO:

List all the characters that matter, even secondary ones, starting with those who get the most screen time.

WHERE:

Just that.

TIME & WEATHER:

An important part of Setting to begin figuring into your vision of the scene.

OPENING:

What's going on during the first paragraph of the scene. If you plan on opening with setting description, note what the people are doing.

PEAK EMOTIONAL MOMENT:

Every great scene has a moment when emotions, tension, and conflict are at their highest, usually anywhere in the second half of the scene. When your imagination conjures up a cool scene, often you're already thinking of that peak moment. It's the main goal of the scene. The rest of the scene serves this moment.

ENDING:

What are the characters doing at the end.

In Opening, Peak Emotional Moment, and Ending, you've created three dots. The rest of the scene outline will be connecting these dots.

SCENE CHECKLISTS

Here's a brief review of each scene type and the checklists for each. Scrivener users will find the scene checklists in Inspector. Excel users will see it in the middle of the scene sheet.

FIRST SCENE CHECKLIST

The first scene in your novel has a lot of work to do. It's the one requiring more work than any other scene. If it doesn't do its job well, none of the other scenes will be read. No one can overestimate its importance.

✓ Introduce your POV's voice and the initial disturbance simultaneously, almost immediately.

You thought about this in "Story Brainstorm." Provide tension to hook your reader in the first pages. At the same time, let the reader know who the novel is about, what kind of a person he/she is. If your first scene is not about your protagonist (and you better have a good reason for that), the reader still needs a great hook.

✓ Establish a distinct, rich setting.

Suck the reader into the novel's world quickly. In fact, grounding the reader early is always appreciated.

✓ Use the imagery (preferably unusually beautiful or strange) to introduce theme and its first challenge.

You should know your novel's theme by now. Put it into your first scene. Don't hide it. Be crafty, of course, but let your reader know what they're getting into. Challenging the theme with gripping imagery in the final paragraphs of the first scene is a great way.

✓ Keep a tight pace.

Don't start your novel with exposition, long paragraphs about what's already happened or long descriptions of the setting. Your book won't sell.

Short descriptions, however, are perfect.

Throughout the first scene, keep it moving. Short paragraphs. People doing things. People using their voices. No one should be sitting around thinking about stuff. That's a contemplative scene, which doesn't belong here.

✓ Using subtext, provide a brief glance into your lead character's inner or outer intentions & struggles, history & personality.

In order to keep a tight pace, there's little room to explain everything right away. Use your character's actions to say it. His/her loaded silences and half-truths. You can make your character interesting while holding back the full truth.

Subtext takes practice. The best writers do it well. Start working on it now.

✓ **Offer a representation of the whole novel, including theme.**

Think of the first scene as a marketing tool. A test drive. The reader wants to know what they're getting for their money. Literally. So show them.

✓ **Show your POV make (or has very recently made) a significant decision that leads to more complications.**

Good characters make things happen. They're more than passive actors in a changing world. An interesting novel, therefore, is full of people who actively cause their own complications, for better or worse, who are "agents of change."

This isn't a main plot's catalyst (or inciting incident, depending on your lingo) but something happening. Right off the bat.

✓ **End with the POV in trouble, prompting the reader to keep reading.**

This is called a prompt. The last paragraphs of any scene should never be a convenient place to put your book down. Get your reader to turn the page to the next scene. How do you do that? Tension. Conflict. Suspense.

ACTION SCENE CHECKLIST:

Action scenes occur when characters do lots of stuff without much explanation to the reader. They encompass more than car chases and gunfights. They're best after scenes of suspense, contemplation, or dialogue, when important decisions are made. Scenes of suspense, contemplation, and dialogue set the dominoes up. Action scenes knock them down.

✓ **Real time feel.**

Skimping on exposition, inner dialogue, and description helps the reader feel like they're in the action. That's good.

✓ Actions tend to be instinctual, revealing character flaws and hidden traits.

Action scenes are the culmination of tension and suspense, so characters often reveal more about themselves than they mean to. Remember when you brainstormed about your character's mask coming down during times of duress? That's an important idea behind action scenes.

This isn't just about negative traits. Tension can bring out the best in us too. Random acts of kindness. Saving a good guy. Saving a bad guy. Saving a cat.

If your action scenes don't have interesting revelations about characters, what's the point? Action for action's sake? This is called an empty "plot device," events that merely move the plot forward without adding to character development. They come off shallow, and you can do better. Even young readers today expect character complications.

Action scenes aren't void of emotions. They're only emotions. Underline that.

✓ POV's arc advances, discovering something about self that rational behavior wouldn't reveal.

Same idea as above. Action scenes are full of change.

✓ The consequences of the actions propel the plot.

As is sounds.

✓ Ending is either a contemplative slow-down or note of high anxiety (page-turner).

End the scene with space for the reader to take a deep breath.

Or hit 'em with a cliffhanger if the next scene in the same plot-line is also an action scene.

Too many action scenes back-to-back become wearisome, however. Some authors alternate subplots to break things up.

DIALOGUE SCENE CHECKLIST:

Lots of scenes are dialogue heavy when the conversation is the most important thing going on. Make the dialogue work hard. Smack as many birds as possible with as few stones as you can.

✓ Ground your reader in the setting early.

Don't forget your reader likes to know where and when, the sooner the better.

✓ Reveal significant personality traits of characters.

Conversations reveal a lot about people. Make sure that happens in your dialogue scenes.

✓ Characters use subtext (ie half-truths, unspoken implications).

Lame dialogue is when everyone says what they're thinking while answering each other's questions directly.

"Hi, honey," Sofia said. "How was your day? You don't seem your usual miserable self. I missed you."

Ethan smiled. "You're late for dinner."

Tension feels more tension-y when the reader picks up on it without you spelling it out for them.

✓ Create tension with verbal and/or subtextual tug-of-war.

No scene should be without some sort of tension or conflict. Even two best friends trying to chose which movie to see. If there's no tension, skip the scene.

Verbal tug-of-war is super fun to write, especially when no one is saying what they really mean.

✓ Use setting, theme, or imagery to control pacing.

You need to include setting, theme, or other kinds of imagery. So insert them between lines of dialogue to control the flow of the scene. Refrain from writing "Ethan paused. Then said..." Instead, have Ethan imagine what his ex-wife would have thought about the view of the moon, then speak.

✓ Reveal significant plot info near end of scene.

The dialogue needs to lead to something. If a character drops a verbal bomb, it should be near the end.

✓ Eliminate any verbal info-dumps.

Using a character to inform the reader about a lengthy history and background of the story will make every reader cringe. And yet, this happens all the time. Then again, it's better for your reader to learn about things from your characters than from you, the narrator.

Think of it this way, most people in real conversations don't speak more than three sentences at a time. That's a good guide.

✓ End with POV either focused on revelation, destabilized by revelation, or starting to take action because of revelation.

Something has been revealed during the scene. Shift gears at the end. Allow the POV character to react briefly at the end of the scene. Use that brief reaction as a prompt for the reader to keep reading.

SUSPENSE SCENE CHECKLIST:

Every genre of novel needs plenty of suspense. Wanna know what you call a beautifully written novel without lots of suspense? Boring.

Apply suspense scenes liberally.

✔ **Open in an uneasy or anxiety-provoking way.**

You can do this with setting, imagery, or an unfortunate event. Let your reader know this is a suspenseful scene right off. Readers love, love, love suspense scenes. Even in slower, literary dramas. So clue them in at the beginning, and they'll happily go there with you.

✔ **Throw POV quickly into trouble.**

Same idea. Most scenes average 1500 words. There's not a lot of space to hem and haw. Create initial trouble in the first page of the scene. Use the rest of it to pull and push on the reader's emotions.

✔ **Add emotional intensity via mood, setting, or sensory details (i.e. weather, decay, touch, color, & light).**

Just as it sounds. Suspense scenes unfold slowly because you're withholding resolution. Use relevant details to slow things down.

✔ **Increase danger mid-scene via POV's own decision.**

Don't let your character be a passive recipient of trouble. The reader will be more engaged if things go from bad to worse because your character is doing things: "Don't go in that house!"

Don't use clichés, however. But you get what I mean.

✔ **Increase danger via the inexplicable.**

Instead of using clichés, use events the reader will never see coming. Not only do readers enjoy surprises, inexplicable events and things evoke curiosity. Create questions. Tease the reader for a few chapters.

✓ Delay conclusions.

Suspense is about unresolved tension.

✓   End with either a release of suspension or cliffhanger).

You can't deny the reader the resolution forever. Wrap up the scene with a place for your reader to sigh relief. Or a moment that escalates the tension even more.

Don't string too many suspense scenes together, however. If you end a suspense scene with a cliffhanger, consider following it with an action scene. Your POV character can blow off all that tension.

DRAMATIC SCENE CHECKLIST:

Unlike suspense scenes, a novel should contain only a small handful of dramatic scenes. I'm looking at you, YA writers. These are the tear-jerking scenes that happen in the middle of a story—not the end where resolution plays a part of the teary process. You're asking the reader to feel the big, primary emotions along with your protagonist. It's tough to do, and it requires patient set-up.

If you're looking for a number, I suggest two dramatic scenes in a novel. Make 'em count.

✓   Open slow, then match pace with escalating emotional complications.

Not only do these scenes need to be set up long before they happen in the novel, but the scene itself needs to set up thoughtfully. Go slow.

✓ Open with and maintain emotional foreboding via subtlety & subtext.

Telling a reader what to feel doesn't work. Ever. Reader emotions must be evoked. Think about the details in the scene that can do the evoking for you.

✓ Utilize 1 or more: confrontation, reunion, time limit, crushed expectations, imminent demise.

These are great reasons for a protagonist to experience major, dramatic push & pull. Put them in context of the three demises from "Story Brainstorm."

✓ Immense push & pull...

Dramatic scenes aren't stagnant. Big things are happening on the inside and the outside.

✓ ...causing irrational behavior.

What's a good dramatic scene without someone doing something they don't think all the way through? Big emotions cause us to do things we can't explain. Or that we don't want anyone to see.

✓ End with POV faced with significant decision or complication, furthering plot.

Drama and its consequential irrational behavior are fun ways to explore character flaws and move the story in surprising ways. Don't hold back.

✓ Close with a cool down, *possibly* exposition.

As it says.

✓ Eliminate all melodrama.

Your important dramatic scene will be ruined if you use obvious attempts to evoke emotions. It's like begging. Lame.

Trouble is, beginning writers have a difficult time identifying melodrama in their scenes because they're not yet proficient with subtext. For some, catching melodrama is harder than catching typos. Have someone else take a look at your scene. Tell them plainly, "Help me remove cheesy melodrama."

Cheesy melodrama never made a reader cry, except with laughter.

✓ Create a powerful emotional reaction in the reader!

Yep. That's the goal.

CONTEMPLATIVE SCENE CHECKLIST:

Contemplative scenes work best after action. It's time for some good ol' quality me time.

✓ Open with either internal monologue, setting/imagery, or transitional action.

Transitional is the key word. Let your reader know it's time to reflect.

✓ Get as intimate, secretive, or ugly as possible.

The reader is going to follow your character's thoughts down the rabbit hole. What's down there? It better contain a few things that make the reader sit up.

✓ Contemplation is a dramatic push/pull about a significant recent plot point or, better, one that's about to occur.

Avoid passages that merely show the character's thought process. Make it relevant to the plot.

✓ Maintain imminent danger during scene.

Here's a good one.

A great contemplative scene is more than your character out for a walk in the sunshine, figuring stuff out. How about figuring stuff out alone in an abandoned park? At night? With the patter of footsteps some-where out there in the dark?

Just make sure the threat of one of the demises is there. If it's not phys-ical harm, what about the heavy looming dread of professional collapse?

✓ **Use setting or theme imagery to create an eerie or tense atmosphere, mirroring emotional content.**

Same idea as above. Contemplative scenes aren't an excuse to write a boring scene.

✓ **End with an energetic prompt toward action, perhaps an action cliffhanger.**

Finish with variety, a shift from slower contemplation to a quickened pace. As always, prompt your reader to go right to the next scene.

FLASHBACK SCENE CHECKLIST:

You can use flashbacks to run a parallel subplot occurring in a different time. Or you can use them to fill in events and emotional content. With the latter, keep them fresh by doing so sparingly.

✓ **The transition to the flashback is unambiguous.**

Make it clear to the reader.

✓ **The flashback has purpose: specific action, specific information, and/or specific relationships. The purpose is obvious and focused.**

Readers resent unnecessary flashbacks because they're pulled from the story they care about. Make sure the flashback has a good reason to exist and the reader knows what that reason is.

✓ The flashback scene contains: setting, action, characters, relevant plot information, and dramatic tension.

Flashback scenes shouldn't be vignettes. They need to be treated as legitimate scenes with all the parts.

✓ If the flashback is a character's memory, the scene should distort the memory given the character's warped emotional lens.

Should the reader trust the memory of your character? How can you clue in the reader that the flashback memory isn't perfect?

✓ The scene is brief (unless running parallel plots).

Since you're pulling the reader out of the story, you should get them back in it as soon as possible.

✓ Give the reader answers. Create more questions. Be a tease.

That's how you keep flashbacks entertaining.

✓ The transition back to the main timeline is unambiguous.

EPIPHANY SCENE CHECKLIST:

Epiphany scenes are another type to use sparingly. These are the big a-ha moments in a novel. You could get away with just one, if you want. I'd put it in the Self-Reflective Mid-Point. Another might do well just before The Final Battle.

Epiphany scenes aren't about figuring out ways to overcome the opposition. They're about understanding personal flaws.

✓ Open with tension, anxiety, irrational behavior,

and/or setting details that mirror the epiphany to come.

Start setting the stage for the epiphany in the first paragraph.

✓ The epiphany is a direct, inescapable result of plot events.

Epiphanies can seem random. They never are.

✓ Up the ante mid-scene with a realization of: threat of loss, irrefutable evidence that shakes status quo further, injury to loved one, or physical danger.

Since you're using an entire scene for the epiphany, make it complicated, multilayered. Let it unfold in stages throughout the scene. Maybe in unsettling ways.

✓ The epiphany should be a surprise to POV, not necessarily the reader.

It's okay that the reader sees the light before your protagonist. That way, the reader can cheer him/her onward. Then again, you don't want your reader having to wait around too long for your characters to figure out the obvious. That's frustrating.

How about this? The protagonist finally realizes something the reader figured out twenty pages ago. Then, the character takes that same realization to a disturbing level the reader didn't see coming. There. Everyone's happy.

✓ The epiphany carries a cost: letting go of expectations, ego, or protective boundaries around a character's flaw.

Overcoming a major flaw can't be easy. Your protagonist figures out how to live life fully, but at the same time figures out how difficult it's going to be to overcome the flaw that's been holding him/her back this whole time.

In terms of story, your character gets ahead, then experiences a setback. That's how stories work. Even in epiphany scenes.

✓ The epiphany morally obligates POV to make a choice, now or later but is at least foreshadowed.

Same idea as above. Once the protagonist gains the epiphany, there's no getting rid of it. Now he/she must act on the revelation. Careful what you wish for. This creates a point of no return, driving your story forward.

✓ Limit narrative summary that explains the epiphany to the reader.

You don't want to be too ambiguous, but as you've now heard a number of ways, you don't want to beat the reader over the head with information. Give the reader fodder to chew on, creating reader participation in the revelation moment.

CLIMACTIC SCENE CHECKLIST:

You get one shot at the climactic scene. Its purpose is so specific I'll be brief here. I don't even need to explain the checklist. It speaks for itself.

By the way, it's the last scene of The Final Battle plot point.

✓ The stakes have already been set up to be explicitly at their highest.

✓ This is the *one* scene of greatest emotional intensity.

✓ The lead character triumphantly overcomes his/her flaw in order to overcome opposition.

✓ The pace is quick and action-oriented.

✓ **There is no exposition.**

✓ **There is a clear winner.**

FINAL SCENE CHECKLIST:

This scene template is slightly misnamed. It's not only the very last scene in the novel. It's for the entire New Status Quo plot point. You can line three of them up together, all doing the same thing, just in different places with different characters.

Don't rush your final scenes. They're your last chance to make an outstanding impression. As much attention should be spent on them as on the first scene.

✓ **The lead character shows his/her flaw (wound, fear, or misconception) now healed—or is at least in recovery.**

Show it. Don't tell it. In the Act Four questionnaire, you already brainstormed a moment when your protagonist actively does something indicating he/she is on the way to living the good life, flaw free. This can be an ongoing thing, happening over a series of final scenes. Or it can be a sweet, subtle action that only the reader will notice.

✓ **Unanswered questions and subplots are resolved— without lengthy exposition.**

Unresolved subplots frustrate readers. Even a few sentences are better than loose strings.

✓ **Emotional resolution is gift-wrapped for the reader, especially in the final pages.**

Artfully guide the reader through the last stages of novel's emotional story.

✓   **The novel's theme is reviewed and clearly championed.**

Review your novel' s message. How'd it go? Did love conquer all? Did blood prove to be thicker than water? The answer should be obvious, but find a meaningful way to sum it up, giving the reader a memorable take away passage.

There are some literary masters who pull off thematic ambiguity. Cormac McCarthy, anyone? They're the source of late night debates and well-researched college term papers. And if you think people will write college term papers about you, great. Be my guest. The world is your oyster.

All those checklists should've opened up your imagination a little more. There's a lot of possibilities that can take a mediocre, predictable scene into a deeply stirring moment in your novel. Hopefully, you learned the possible complexities of each scene type, spurring your imagination to better storytelling.

Next we'll review the more fundamental questionnaire you'll be filling out for every scene. Just about every scene will have the same questions. Your answers will be the building blocks of your scene outlines.

SCENE BASICS

You'll see all the questions in past tense. Originally, they were in present tense. However, that led to my own answers being present tense. Then, when I copy/pasted my answers into a scene outline, the outline was also present tense, creating an extra step and some fussing up for my little brain. Hence, most questions in the Fool Proof Outline, beginning to end, are in past tense for that reason.

If you're writing a novel in present tense, your answers should also be present tense.

Try to use single, complete sentences.

Here's the Fool Proof Outline's steps for outlining a scene.

- Lock in the basics you need to know about about every scene you ever write. I call them "Scene Basics." Clever.
- Sketch a rough play-by-play, establishing the scene's major action beats.
- Identify the most important aspects of the scene's setting.

- Identify specific changes in character & plot that the scene advances.
- Brainstorm specific details to increase tension.
- Sketch another play-by-play, this time longer, including more details.
- Copy/paste all these details into a chronological outline within your writing space.

SCENE BASICS

WHO WAS THE POV CHARACTER?

Beginning writers "switch heads" without even realizing it. It's distracting. Everything about a scene needs to be conveyed through the perspective of a single character. Doesn't have to be your protagonist, either, even if the protagonist is in the scene.

At any rate, you need to pick a character as your POV and stick with him/her all the way through to the end of the scene.

You might ask, "But what if I'm writing in Third Person Omniscient?"

To which I'd say, "Don't. This isn't the 19th century, and it never will be."

WHAT WAS POV DOING AT THE BEGINNING?

You identified this in the synopsis.

WHAT DID POV NEED?

Every scene is built around a POV character with a goal. Make it clear for best results.

LIST THE OTHER CHARACTERS IN THE SCENE, ALONG WITH THEIR WANTS DURING THE SCENE?

Vonnegut reminded us every character wants something, even if it's a glass of water. That's going to affect scene subtext.

WHO OR WHAT OBSTRUCTED POV'S NEED?

Every POV with a goal needs something or someone trying to jack it all up. That's called conflict.

LIST THE TIMES THIS HAPPENS:

In this one scene. Two or three times is all a scene can handle, depending on the nature of the conflict.

WHAT WAS THE MOMENT & EMOTION OF PEAK INTENSITY?

This is the most important moment in each scene. It can happen anytime within it. All things before lead toward it. All things after lead away from it.

WHAT CONCERNS WERE RAISED BY THE END?

No scene should end on an anxiety-free note. None. Except final scenes.

WHAT WAS POV DOING AT THE END, SHOWING THAT CONCERN?

The last actions of the scene give you the last dot to connect.

SCENE PLAY-BY-PLAY #1

LIST THE MAJOR ACTION BEATS:

Most scenes can have three to eight action beats. Using your answers above, list the scene's beats chronologically.

Now, you just created a good, simple outline for this scene. Well done. Keep going to make it great.

VISUALIZE THE SCENE THROUGH POV'S EYES, INCLUDING ALL THE ABOVE.

Literally close your eyes. Put on appropriate music. Now, go into movie mode and imagine you're the POV. Replay it as much as you want. I love this part.

THEN, IN ~250 WORDS OF THE SIMPLEST LANGUAGE POSSIBLE, SUMMARIZE THE SCENE:

When I say simplest language, I mean it. Use ridiculously plain sentences, like you'd see in a 1st Grade reader. Avoid sentences with commas. Avoid grammar complexities that cause you to self-edit.

Follow the scene while in movie mode, pause the projector, and write down some details. Mostly just the movement of people and things. Don't bother yet with thoughts and feelings.

*I got this idea from Rachel Aaron's **2k to 10k: Writing Faster, Writing Better, and Writing More of What You Love**. Trying to figure out what you're going to write while in the process of writing is a terrible idea. Knowing what you're going to write before you write is waaaay better. Which is why outlines work so well for us.*

As a side note, this is when dictation software begins paying for itself. I simply close my eyes, headphones on, and slowly dictate the simplified mental movie into a voice recorder. Takes practice, sure, but I'd never do it any other way.

SETTING

BRAINSTORM VIVID DETAILS THAT SHOW TIME, PLACE, WEATHER, & CULTURE *FROM POV'S PERSPECTIVE*:

The key here is "from POV's perspective." Every description of setting should also reveal something about the character. Word choices. Cultural judgements. Mood. All sorts of character variables affect setting descriptions.

LIST AT LEAST A FEW MOMENTS WHEN POV PHYSICALLY INTERACTED WITH THE ENVIRONMENT:

Make sure setting is more than wallpaper. You already brainstormed setting ideas in "Story Brainstorm." Revisit them. Setting should be a part of the active movements of your characters. This brings the environment to life.

WHAT SETTING DETAILS MIRRORED THE TENSION AND/OR THEME?

Motifs. Imagery. Symbols. Don't worry about being obvious to the reader.

In real life, we notice details around us relevant to our predicaments. It can be uncanny, and we're tempted to see them as signs from beyond. Maybe they are. But it's not bizarre for characters to pick up on environmental details that speak to their story. Actually, it's often great writing.

WHAT OBJECTS REVEALED DETAILS ABOUT PLOT & CHARACTER?

Important recurring objects can also be motifs.

Or sometimes a little item falls into the spotlight for a moment, and it tells us things. You can learn a lot about a woman by the deodorant she wears and where she buys her underwear.

LIST A FEW MUNDANE DETAILS THAT ENGAGED POV'S SENSES, CREATING A SENSE OF REALISM:

Writers often skip the mundane details. Smells, for instance, are only mentioned when they're important to the plot. Including little sensual details others might overlook add to a scene's mood and realism.

Don't overdo it. But dabble thoughtfully.

CHARACTERS & PLOT

HOW DID POV *ACTIVELY* MOVE THE PLOT FORWARD?

Articulate how the character is an "agent of change," not merely a passive dupe.

LIST SPECIFIC VISCERAL/SOMATIC RESPONSES TO EMOTIONS OR ACTIONS, *ESPECIALLY* FOR THE MOMENT OF PEAK INTENSITY:

Showing emotions can be tricky. It's still better than merely telling the reader how a character feels.

Showing can include internal or invisible manifestations of emotions, like rising temperature, shallow breath, or a pounding heart.

Keep in mind, showing an emotion doesn't guarantee the reader will feel it too.

*I often keep my Kindle version of Ackerman & Puglisi's **The Emotional Thesaurus** actually split screened as I outline my scenes. It's a solid resource for this stuff.*

HOW DID POV'S CHARACTER FLAW SHOW UP?

The flaw should be in there. It's always around. Maybe in big ways. But more likely, in small, hard to pin down behaviors.

HOW WAS POV FORCED TO REEVALUATE OR CHANGE?

Small evolutions throughout a novel are believable. One big, permanent change right after an epiphany isn't, which, truth be told, never happens in real life.

DRAMATIC TENSION

HOW DID DANGER OR DEMISE LOOM (PHYSICAL, PSYCHOLOGICAL, OR PROFESSIONAL)?

Back to the looming demise(s) plaguing your characters throughout the novel. Think they ever get a break? Nope. On some level, even if it's unconsciously gnawing on the brain, the threat of demise has to be in there.

BRAINSTORM AT LEAST TWO UNEXPECTED WAYS TO SHOW TENSION IN THE SCENE:

Surprise yourself. Think outside the box. Imagine something so intense it would never happen in this novel. Great. Use some variation of it.

SCENE PLAY-BY-PLAY #2

IMAGINE THE SCENE THROUGH ALL 5 OF POV'S SENSES.

Get back into movie mode. This time, you've got surround sound. And a rumble seat.

Are you thoroughly aware of the relevant details of this scene.

TWEAK SETTING QUESTIONS ABOVE IF NEEDED.

Any new setting details come up?

THEN, IN ~500 WORDS OF THE SIMPLEST LANGUAGE POSSIBLE, SUMMARIZE THE SCENE:

I know 500 words for a sketch sounds like a lot. But it doesn't need to be in chronological order. Just start jotting things down. Follow your action beats as best you can, but don't get hung up.

Basically, you're doing a stream of consciousness exercise with all the details you've come up with so far. No pressure.

If it feels like too much effort, you're thinking too much, probably in the form of self-editing as you type. That's bad. No one will ever read these sketches. No one will see the misspellings and lousy word choices. The best thing to come out of these sketches is your ability to write without your inner critic. The second best thing will be a solid grasp on your scenes.

EXTRA STUFF

WHAT OPENING HOOK LURED POV (AND READER) DEEPER INTO THE SCENE?

Something on the scene's first page should make the rest irresistible.

WHAT WAS THE PROMPT TO THE NEXT SCENE?

Something in the scene's last paragraph should keep the spark of interest alive in the reader.

"Hey, sweetie? That light gonna be out anytime soon?"

"Soon as I finish this chapter, k?"

"You said that, like, four chapters ago."

Bingo.

WHAT FASCINATING IDEA, FACT, OR EVENT WAS TEASED TO COME LATER, EVEN SUBTLY?

Sales literature does this. It keeps talking up the big secret, listing all the benefits, recounting all the testimonials, the whole time assuring you the big reveal is coming right up.

With fiction you can do the same thing. Except your reveal will be awesome. And the teasing is half the fun for the reader. Instead of teasing the climax, pick something that's a few scenes away, something specific to your genre. Tease that. Repeat. That way, the reader will enjoy the tease knowing something cool really is, after all, coming right up.

WHAT SPECIFIC ACTIONS FURTHERED SUBPLOTS, W/O BEING MERE EXPOSITION OR AN INFO-DUMP?

Keep your subplots planned. Find ways for subplots and your primary plot to have a significant effect on each other.

WHAT WAS THE UNEXPLAINED, UNEXPECTED EVENT, ACTION, OR ITEM THAT WILL SURPRISE THE READER?

Make sure every scene has something truly unpredictable. Unpredictable events make the story your own. No one else would have thought of them.

HOW WAS THE THEME CHALLENGED OR CHAMPIONED?

Articulate this as a complete, clear sentence.

Everyone has their own process. I end up with less backtracking and rewriting if I fill out this questionnaire for every scene in the novel before moving on. Most, if not all, of your own doubts and insecurities will find resolution before the next final steps.

Up to this point, the Fool Proof Outline has laid out what you need to produce a fantastic novel. If something somewhere is still eating at you—maybe you don't know what yet—review your work so far. The answer is in there, lingering in one of the brainstorms. Work it out now, before locking your outline into place.

PART 5

WRITING THE 1ST DRAFT

SNAPPING THINGS IN PLACE

This part of the Fool Proof Outline is so ridiculously fun I can't stand it.

Get your copy/paste fingers warmed up.

Start with your action beats listed in Scene Play-By-Play #1. Copy/paste them in the writing space of the scene. (Excel users have a text box ready to go in the middle of the sheet.) Leave a few lines of space between each action beat, making it easier to paste between them as you go.

You now have a rudimentary outline for the scene. Knowing what you know about the scene, you could simply write your 1st Draft now, and it'd be great.

But make sure you don't leave anything out. How? By copy/pasting the rest of the details directly into your outline.

Go to the very top of the scene questionnaire. Start working your way down, copy/pasting details where you feel they'll fit appropriately into your outline.

Each detail should be its own line. You can combine them into coherent paragraphs later when you write your 1st Draft.

Don't worry about perfection. You can move things around later. Setting details. Character details. All of it. Slide them right into your outline chronologically.

You can repeat details throughout the outline, too, if you want. When you write your 1st Draft, you'll be rewording everything anyway.

By the way, don't **cut**/paste. Copy. That way your original notes will always remain intact. They'll come in handy later when you tinker.

The only things that don't get moved over are your 250 and 500 word sketches. Those were just practice. Because they're not moved over, you might become tempted to skip doing them at all later. I started skipping them, and found myself hung up during the drafting process. Then, I returned to doing them, and 1st Drafts came easily again. Coincidence?

Once you've copy/pasted all your details into your writing space, you have a chronological outline, running top to bottom, containing everything your scene needs. Some lines will be complete sentences. Some will be single, simple phrases. That's fine. Some details, even important ones, only need to be a simple phrase, nestled within a longer sentence later.

You may even copy/paste items from the "Scene Checklist." I do. Not all of them. But some. They help me include important scene components as I write my 1st Draft.

Done?

You scene is now thoroughly outlined.

After doing this a few times with a few scenes, email me at scrivenertemplates@gmail.com. What are your thoughts? How fool proof was it?

YOUR FIRST DRAFT

Repeat after me:

"My 1st Draft will suck."

"No one will ever, ever, ever, ever read it."

"A terrible 1st Draft is better than no 1st Draft."

Great job.

Depending on your process, you can write a scene's 1st Draft right after you construct its outline or you can outline every scene and write the novel's entire 1st Draft all at once.

Me? I outline every scene. Tinker. Then, I draft each scene one at time. A few a day. Why? Because a scene is somewhere around 1500 words. Drafting 1500 words is less intimidating than drafting 55,000 words. I can do 1500 easy-peasy.

Either way.

You're still going to draft your novel one scene at a time. So pick one scene's outline. Review it. Now, let's turn it into a 1st Draft.

You now have one heck of a connect-the-dots in front of you. With more experience, you'll begin seeing the 1st Draft just by looking at the outline, the invisible lines between the dots. It's all there. Just. Connect. The. Dots.

In Scrivener, I write my 1st Draft directly below the outline, split-screening the editor, outline on top, draft on bottom. You can organize your own screen however you like, even cut/pasting the outline into a separate text box or document. You'll figure out what works best for you.

Writing is still work. Even writing while following the Fool Proof Outline you constructed for each scene takes effort. The title of the system is Fool Proof Outline, not Easy Way Out Outline.

Will you still struggle? At times, sure. But you've now begun using a system of exploration and creativity that should eliminate writer's block for you. "What do I write next?" Connect the dots.

You say, "But my 1st Draft sounds clunky and amateurish this way!"

Yeah, but you'll get better. Because you're a writer. And you stay at it. Repeat the mantras above. Keep writing.

If this isn't your first novel, you know that editing and rewriting a draft is a whole other process. But you can't begin to edit or rewrite until you have a big block of clay to work with. [*As an example, I'll leave in that mixed metaphor just for you.*]

That about wraps things up on this end. On the next pages, you'll find a link to the Fool Proof Outline site where you can reach out to me with questions and comments. Please do.

I wish you all the best in your writing. It's hard work, but we're all on the same team. We can lean on each other now and then. You have my outlining system now. You can lean on it whenever you want.

Please leave a review on Amazon if you have the time and an opinion. Other writers will want to know what you think!

All the best,

Christopher

PS Ready to rocket your daily word counts? ***Fool Proof Dictation*** is the only book of its kind, teaching you to train your brain for enjoyable and productive dictation!

Now available!

THE TEMPLATES YOU'LL NEED

The template files are downloadable from Dropbox.

Go to the Fool Proof Outline site:

foolproofoutline.wordpress.com

You'll find the links there, both the Scrivener and Excel files. No sweat.

I'll also post outline & drafting related updates as it goes on the Fool Proof Outline blog, same web address. You'll get to see early all my brainstorms, outlines, and drafts in action. And then you can make all the comments you want. I'll even take encouragement now and then!

Whatever help I can give you, just ask on the site! Or you can email me directly at *scrivenertemplates@gmail.com*.

Be well.

Printed in Great Britain
by Amazon

76871573R00066